ld:

down

A & C Black • London

Produced for A & C Black by
Monkey Puzzle Media Ltd
48 York Avenue
Hove BN3 1PJ, UK

MONKEY PUZZLE MEDIA LTD

Published by A & C Black Publishers Limited
36 Soho Square, London W1D 3QY

Paperback published 2009
First published 2008
Copyright © 2008 A & C Black Publishers Limited

ISBN 978-1-4081-0027-1 (hardback)
ISBN 978-1-4081-0121-6 (paperback)

The right of Sean Callery to be identified as the
author of this Work has been asserted by him in
accordance with the Copyright, Designs and Patents
Act 1988.

A CIP catalogue record for this book is available
from the British Library.

Editor: Cath Senker
Design: Mayer Media Ltd
Picture research: Lynda Lines
Series consultant: Jane Turner

This book is produced using paper that is made
from wood grown in managed, sustainable forests.
It is natural, renewable and recyclable. The logging
and manufacturing processes conform to the
environmental regulations of the country of origin.

Printed in China by C & C Offset Printing Co., Ltd

Picture acknowledgements
Corbis pp. 18 (Roger Tidman), 23 (Vincent Laforet);
FLPA p. 11 (Frans Lanting); Getty Images pp. 16 (Pal
Hermansen), 21 (Pete Ryan), 24 (AFP); MPM Images
pp. 6 (Digital Vision), 17; NASA/Goddard Space
Flight Center pp. 12, 13, 15; Panos Pictures pp. 4
(Dieter Telemans), 22 (Dieter Telemans);
Photolibrary.com pp. 1 (AlaskaStock), 8 bottom
(Urf Urf/F1 Online), 14 (Scott Winer/OSF), 19
(AlaskaStock), 29 (Bengt af Geljerstam/Scanpix);
Picasa p. 7 (Tushar); Science Photo Library pp. 5
(Tom Van Sant/Geosphere Project, Santa Monica),
25 (NASA), 26 (British Antarctic Survey), 28 (P G
Adam/Publiophoto Diffusion); Still Pictures pp. 8 top
(Joerg Boethling), 9 (Ullstein-Oberhaeuser/CARO),
10 (Mark Edwards), 27 (Mark Shenley); UAF p. 20
(Marmian Grimes).

The front cover shows a polar bear standing on
pack ice (Getty Images/Paul Miles).

Every effort has been made to contact copyright
holders of material reproduced in this book. Any
omissions will be rectified in subsequent printings if
notice is given to the publishers.

CONTENTS

Abbreviations **C** stands for Centigrade • **F** stands for Fahrenheit • **ft** stands for feet • **m** stands for metres • **kg** stands for kilograms • **lb** stands for pounds

Sea change

London. New York. Hong Kong. Tokyo. No – it's not a list of great places for holidays. These cities could be flooded if sea levels carry on rising.

The Earth is getting hotter. As a result, sea levels have risen by 15–20 centimetres (up to 8 inches) in 100 years. They could rise by another metre (3 feet) by 2100. That's a lot of extra sea water. It spells trouble for people in low-lying countries such as Bangladesh. Millions of homes could disappear under water.

Double heat

Global temperatures have risen by about 1 degree Centigrade (1.8 degrees Fahrenheit) over the last century. The **polar regions** warmed by at least double that amount. It doesn't sound much, but this polar meltdown is a massive change for the planet.

In Bangladesh, 15 million people live less than a metre (3 ft) above sea level. They already often suffer from floods.

polar region areas of the globe surrounding the North and South Pole

Arctic

More than 70 per cent of the Earth's surface is covered by water or ice.

Water **expands** when it is warm. When the temperature rises, so do water levels.

Heat **melts** ice and it flows as water into the seas.

Antarctic

Heating up

There is life on Earth because our planet is just the right distance from the Sun. Much nearer and we'd sizzle like a burger on a barbecue. Any further away and we'd freeze like an ice cube.

Keeping warm

Without greenhouse gases, the planet would be about 30 degrees Centigrade (54 degrees Fahrenheit) cooler – too cold for most life.

The Earth is surrounded by layers of gases that stop heat from escaping. This is called the greenhouse effect. It helps keep the Earth at the right temperature for us to live. The main greenhouse gases are **water vapour**, carbon dioxide, methane and nitrous oxide.

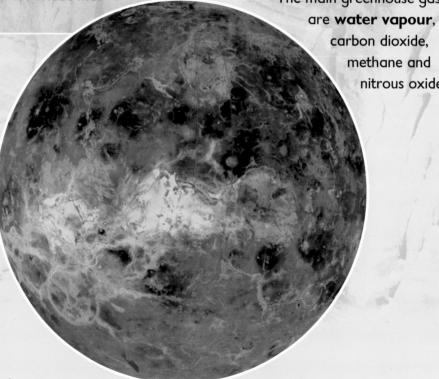

*The planet Venus once had a **climate** rather like ours. A build-up of greenhouse gases boosted its temperature to twice that of a hot oven.*

climate long-term weather pattern   **water vapour** water in the form of gas

The trouble is, human activity makes huge amounts of carbon dioxide, methane and nitrous oxide. These gases collect in the **atmosphere**. The extra trapped heat is warming up the planet.

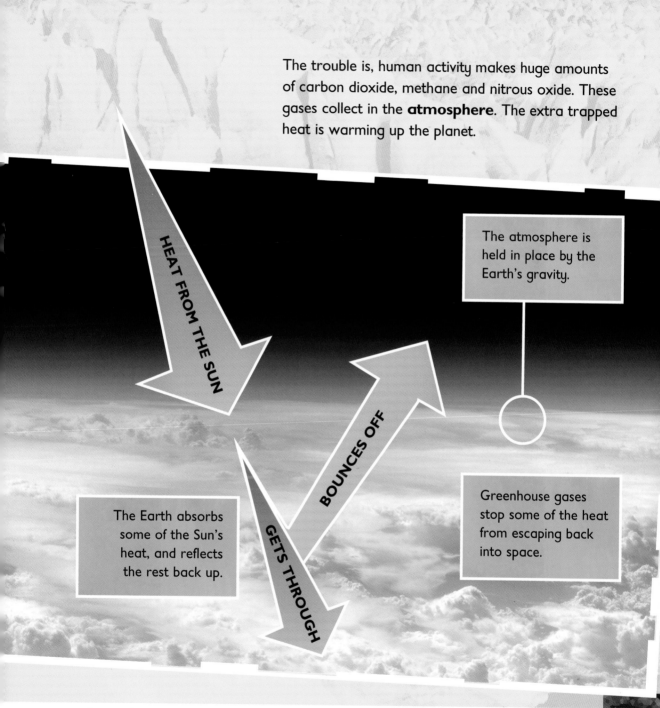

HEAT FROM THE SUN

BOUNCES OFF

GETS THROUGH

The atmosphere is held in place by the Earth's gravity.

The Earth absorbs some of the Sun's heat, and reflects the rest back up.

Greenhouse gases stop some of the heat from escaping back into space.

atmosphere   layers of gases around the Earth

Who did it?

Each year, people pump out nearly 8 billion tonnes (9 billion tons) of carbon dioxide into the atmosphere. Who is to blame?

Paarp!

Burp!

*The nitrogen in farm **fertilizers** used to grow crops creates nitrous oxide.*

Methane makers

Cows and sheep let out the greenhouse gas methane when they burp and fart. Most of it comes out of the front and not the rear end.

fertilizer   substance spread on crops to help them to grow

On average, each person in the world creates 3.7 tonnes (4 tons) of carbon dioxide every year. People in rich countries create far more than those in poor countries. Indonesians make 2 tonnes (2.2 tons) a year, but each American produces more than 20 tonnes (22 tons)!

*Burning **fossil fuels** releases carbon dioxide into the atmosphere. It rises in the air as carbon dioxide gas.*

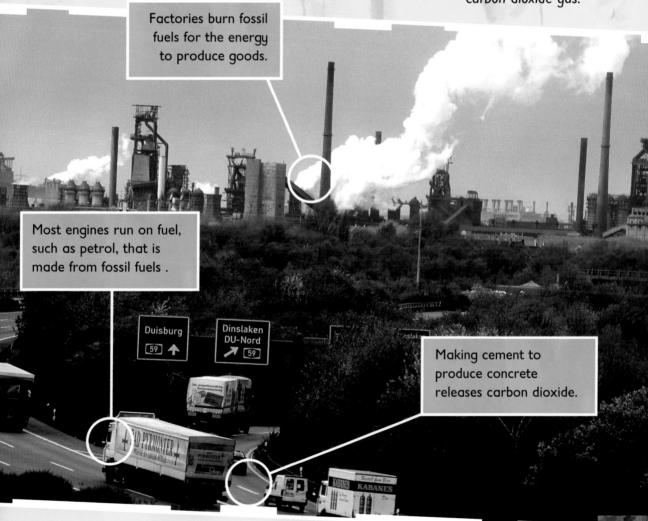

Factories burn fossil fuels for the energy to produce goods.

Most engines run on fuel, such as petrol, that is made from fossil fuels .

Duisburg
59 ↑

Dinslaken
DU-Nord
↗ 59

Making cement to produce concrete releases carbon dioxide.

fossil fuels   coal, oil and gas

Chop till we drop

What has chopping down trees got to do with the warming of the world?

Vast rainforests around the **Equator** help the Earth to cope with greenhouse gases. The trees soak up carbon dioxide and release oxygen. Yet over the last 60 years, about half the world's rainforests have been cut down. With fewer trees, less carbon dioxide is absorbed. The rest escapes into the atmosphere.

People cut down rainforest trees so they can farm the land and use the wood as fuel. When trees are burned, carbon dioxide goes into the atmosphere.

Photosynthesis

Photosynthesis is when plants take in sunlight, water and carbon dioxide to make food and oxygen gas. Animals need this gas to breathe. So photosynthesis is good for plants and good for the rest of the world.

Equator   the imaginary line around the middle of the Earth

The tree uses sunlight to turn carbon dioxide into food.

O_2 O_2 O_2

SUNSHINE

The tree releases oxygen.

Like all plants, the tree takes in carbon dioxide.

Trees store the carbon until they die.

Shrinking ice caps

At the top and bottom of the world are the polar ice caps: huge areas of frozen ice. The ice caps act as giant mirrors, reflecting about one-third of the Sun's rays back into space – and helping to keep the planet cooler.

Cool! Arctic sea ice in 1979

Sea ice in the Arctic is getting thinner. By 2060, there could be no ice there in the summer at all!

Arctic v Antarctic

Even though they look similar, the polar regions really are poles apart. The Arctic is a frozen sea. The Antarctic is land, covered by a huge ice layer. On average, this ice is an incredible 2,000 metres (6,600 feet) deep.

But now that the planet is getting warmer, the ice caps are melting and shrinking. The Arctic ice cap is now 9 per cent smaller than it was 10 years ago. This means that less of the Sun's rays are being reflected back – and the planet is getting even warmer.

Red alert!

Arctic sea ice in 2003

A fresh problem

About 80 per cent of the Maldives are less than 2 m (7 ft) above sea level.

A glacier is a vast mass of freshwater ice like a slow-moving river. It slides downwards until it crashes into the sea.

Glaciers, ice sheets, ice caps, **icebergs** and **ice floes** all form part of the water cycle. They store about three-quarters of the world's fresh water.

As the world warms, the glaciers are shrinking. They either melt, raising sea levels, or collapse into the sea to form icebergs and ice floes.

Water rise

If the whole of the Greenland ice sheet melted, sea levels would rise by 7 metres (23 feet), swamping whole countries.

The Maldives are a group of 1,200 beautiful islands in the Indian Ocean, where tourists love to soak up the sun. A small rise in the water level could wash the Maldives under the ocean forever.

iceberg   huge mass of floating ice, with only 10 per cent visible above the surface

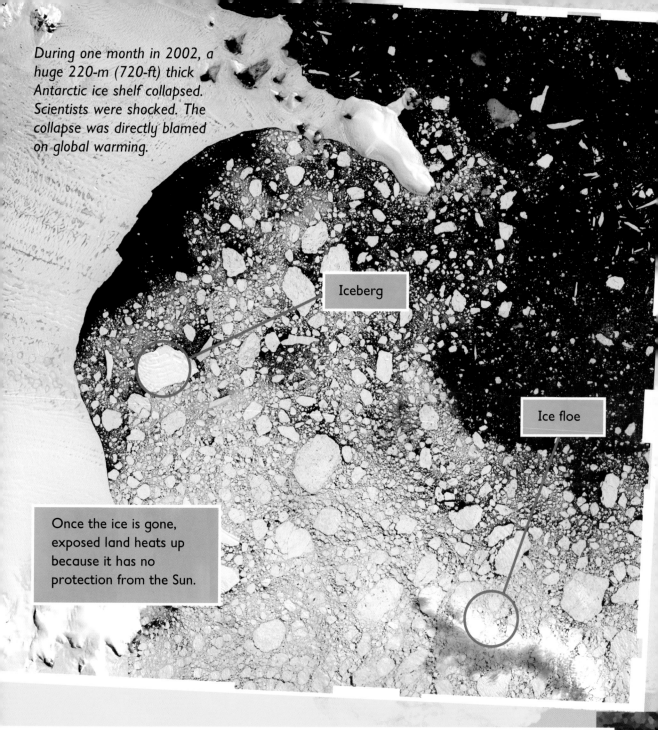

During one month in 2002, a huge 220-m (720-ft) thick Antarctic ice shelf collapsed. Scientists were shocked. The collapse was directly blamed on global warming.

Iceberg

Ice floe

Once the ice is gone, exposed land heats up because it has no protection from the Sun.

ice floe   large area of floating ice

Can't bear it

Polar bears have no natural predators. So why are they dying out?

This polar bear on an ice floe feasts on a seal.

Polar bears swim through the water to reach ice floes where they can rest and hunt ringed seals. As the Arctic sea ice melts, polar bears have fewer places to go. They are forced to swim longer distances.

The warmer weather is a problem too. The bears are used to fasting (going without food) through the summer when there is no ice. Now the temperature stays warmer for longer, so they have to go hungry for longer.

Unbearable diet

Surveys show polar bears are losing weight and having fewer cubs as their habitat shrinks. They lose 10 kilograms (22 pounds) for every week without ice to hunt on.

predator   animal that kills and eats other animals

The polar bears are affected by **pesticides** too. Pesticides from crops flow into rivers and seas. They get into the food chain. First the plankton absorb the pesticides, then fish eat the plankton, and seals eat the fish. So the polar bear's seal dinner contains pesticides.

The dots show how the pesticides become more concentrated as they move up the food chain and end up in the polar bear.

When the polar bear eats the seal, the pesticide has reached the top of the food chain.

Seals eat fish, including the pesticide that has travelled up the food chain.

Many fish eat plankton and absorb the pesticides into their bodies.

The food chain in the Arctic.

Plankton: these tiny plants or animals take in pesticides from the water.

pesticide   chemical used to kill pests that damage plants

Krill killer

It's no bigger than your little finger, but without it much sea life would come to an end. That's krill, a tiny shrimp-like creature. Fish, penguins, seals and whales alike eat it by the mouthful.

Krill shelter under sea ice on the **Antarctic Peninsula**. They live off tiny plants. Since 1970, much of the sea ice has melted, and the krill have lost their habitat. By 2000, 80 per cent had gone.

Emperor penguins are going hungry because of the lack of krill. Also, fisherman take so many fish from the Antarctic that there are few left for penguins to eat. Not only that, but the penguins are losing their nesting sites. These are on the sea ice that is melting. Some penguin **colonies** have halved in size over the last 50 years.

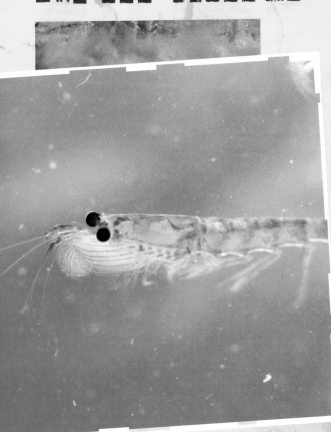

Krill are vital to the food chain in the sea.

In the pink

Sometimes there are so many krill in the water that they turn the sea pink!

Antarctic Peninsula   a section of the Antarctic jutting out to the north

Ice is **melting.**

Emperors are the largest of the penguins.

Emperor penguins lay their eggs on the sea ice, away from the water.

Nowadays, there are fewer krill and fish in the sea.

colony   a group of animals that live together

What a gas

The permafrost is full of methane. Poke a hole in the permafrost, light a match, and the gas goes up in flames!

Imagine your house falling down – because the weather is too warm! That's what is happening in Siberia, Russia. When the frozen ground thaws, whole buildings may collapse.

In the coldest parts of the world, the ground stays frozen all the time. This is called permafrost.

In Siberia, there is a frozen **peat bog** 1 million square kilometres (385,000 square miles) in size. The area has warmed by 3 degrees Centigrade (5.4 degrees Fahrenheit) over the last 40 years. The ice in the peat bog is melting. This is bad news for the people who live there.

Frosty

Did you know that more than a quarter of the world's land is permafrost?

thaws   turns back into water after being frozen   **peat bog**   wet, spongy ground

Rising temperatures are also bad news for the planet because the frozen soil contains around 70 billion tonnes (77 billion tons) of methane, which could be released. Methane is a powerful greenhouse gas that traps 20 times more heat than carbon dioxide.

The permafrost is melting in Canada too. This building in Yukon Territory is sinking.

Whoaa!

Buildings start to fall down.

Water is **frozen** into the permafrost.

When the frost **thaws**, the ground is no longer as solid.

The Earth's revenge?

The Earth's weather patterns are changing into the plot of a disaster movie as we suffer more storms, floods and droughts. Everyone is affected by this.

*Men collecting water from a hole in a dry riverbed in Ethiopia. When there is a **drought**, crops cannot grow and people go hungry.*

"Climate change" is a better way of describing what is happening than "global warming". Our weather is shaped by how much heat is in the atmosphere, and the patterns seem to be changing. Some areas are becoming hotter and drier. Others face violent winds and floods.

Heatwave

Summer 2007 saw an extreme heatwave in southern Europe. Soaring temperatures and severe drought created perfect conditions for fires to spread in Greece. The flames destroyed forests and farmland, killing 84 people.

drought   long period without rain   **hurricane**   severe sea storm with high winds

In 2005, **Hurricane** Katrina hit New Orleans, USA. Afterwards, most of the city was flooded.

Water gushed over the **levees**, the banks that were supposed to hold it back.

The water covered buildings and swept vehicles away.

levee   a bank built along the edges of a river to stop the land from being flooded

Death rays

Did you know that the Earth has its very own sun block called ozone? Yet humans have damaged it.

The layer of ozone gas in the Earth's atmosphere is 20 to 60 kilometres (12 to 40 miles) above ground level. It blocks out the **ultraviolet radiation** that can cause sunburn, skin cancer and death.

In 1985, scientists realized the ozone layer was becoming too thin to do its job. The damage was mostly caused by CFCs, gases that were used in fridges and spray cans for many years. The CFCs attacked the ozone layer. The thinning of the ozone layer is worst over Antarctica.

Although the damage has slowed since CFCs were widely banned in 1995, the effects will last many years. It shows how human actions can harm our environment.

The Sun's rays can harm our skin. That's why it's sensible to wear sun block, sunglasses and a hat.

ultraviolet radiation   invisible rays from the Sun that can cause damage

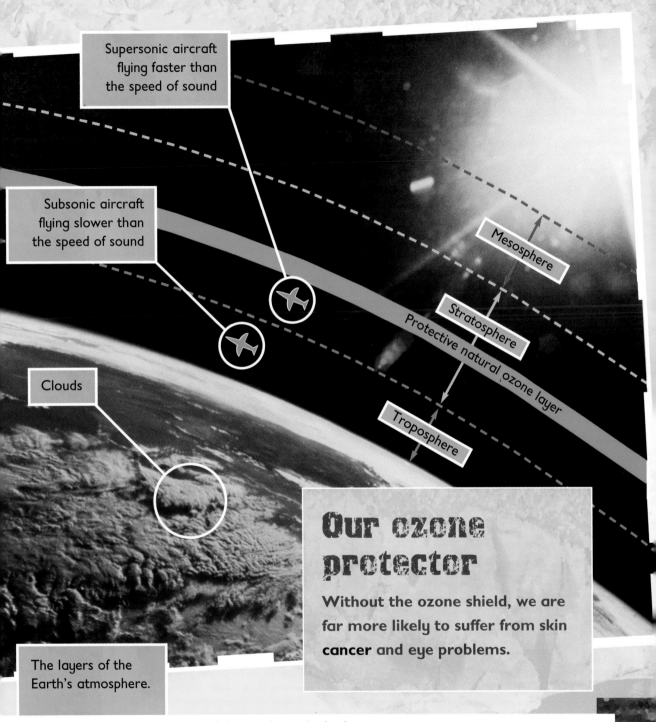

Supersonic aircraft flying faster than the speed of sound

Subsonic aircraft flying slower than the speed of sound

Mesosphere

Stratosphere

Protective natural ozone layer

Troposphere

Clouds

The layers of the Earth's atmosphere.

Our ozone protector

Without the ozone shield, we are far more likely to suffer from skin **cancer** and eye problems.

cancer disease causing harmful growths in the body

Tube journey

Ice ages

The Earth's climate has changed throughout its history. There have been times when average temperatures were either warmer, or colder, than now. Our planet has seen several major **ice ages**, when much of the land was covered by ice.

What can a tube cut deep into the ice tell us about the history of our planet?

Scientists have cut a tube of ice more than 3 kilometres (11,866 feet) long in the Antarctic. It has helped them to work out the temperature of the Earth over the last three-quarters of a million years!

The scientists have shown that the Earth has sometimes been freezing cold. At other times, it has been much warmer. Now, it is warming up fast when it should be cooling down. Human beings have caused this change. What will happen next?

Scientists will examine the air bubbles frozen into the ice tube. They can tell what the atmosphere and climate were like at the time the air bubbles froze.

ice age   one of the long periods of time when much of the Earth was covered in ice

Scientists believe that this century the Earth will change in many ways. There will be more extreme weather. The average temperature will rise between 1 and 6°C (1.8 and 11°F) – higher in the polar regions. Some **species** will die out as their habitat disappears or changes.

MELTING GLACIERS

RISING SEA LEVELS

MELTING ICE SHEETS

RISING SEA LEVELS

MELTING ICE CAPS

RISING SEA LEVELS

species group of similar animals

27

Action!

The bad news is that everybody contributes to climate change. The good news is that everyone can do something about it.

We can use less energy from fossil fuels by following the "three Rs":

*Electricity made from **renewable** energy, such as wind power, is better for the environment than using fossil fuels.*

- **R**educe what you use. In the winter, why not turn down the heating and put on another jumper?

- **R**euse. Fill a water bottle from the tap instead of buying another container. Give away your old toys and clothes instead of throwing them in the bin.

- **R**ecycle materials such as glass, plastic, cans and paper.

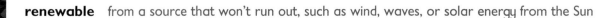

renewable   from a source that won't run out, such as wind, waves, or solar energy from the Sun

Glass can be crushed, then heated and shaped to make new glass.

It is possible to recycle some plastics to make new goods, such as fleeces.

It is easy to recycle paper and cardboard.

Aluminium cans can be melted to make new containers.

Much of this rubbish could be recycled.

Can power

Recycling one aluminium can saves enough energy to run a television for three hours.

Glossary

Antarctic Peninsula a section of the Antarctic jutting out to the north

atmosphere layers of gases around the Earth

cancer disease causing harmful growths in the body

climate long-term weather pattern

colony a group of animals that live together

drought long period without rain

Equator the imaginary line around the middle of the Earth

fertilizer substance spread on crops to help them to grow

fossil fuels coal, oil and gas

hurricane severe sea storm with high winds

ice age one of the long periods of time when much of the Earth was covered in ice

ice floe large area of floating ice

iceberg huge mass of floating ice, with only 10 per cent visible above the surface

levee a bank built along the edges of a river to stop the land from being flooded

peat bog wet, spongy ground

pesticide chemical used to kill pests that damage plants

polar region areas of the globe surrounding the North and South Pole

predator animal that kills and eats other animals

renewable energy from a source that won't run out, such as wind, waves, or solar energy from the Sun

species group of similar animals

thaws turns back into water after being frozen

ultraviolet radiation invisible rays from the Sun that can cause damage

water vapour water in the form of gas

Further information

Books

Funny Weather by Kate Evans (Myriad Editions, 2006)
Fact-packed book with lively and funny illustrations.

I Wonder Why There's a Hole in the Sky by Sean Callery (Kingfisher, 2008)
Basic briefing for young readers on climate change.

You Can Save the Planet by Rich Hough (A&C Black, 2007)
Takes you through the environmental baddies hidden in an average day – from shopping and eating to using mobile phones – and how you can make a difference.

Films

The 11th Hour directed by Nadia Conners and Leila Conners Petersen (Warner Home Video, 2008)
Documentary on the damage being done to the planet's life systems, narrated by Leonardo DiCaprio.

The Day After Tomorrow directed by Roland Emmerich (20th Century Fox, 2007; Certificate 12)
Disaster movie in which massive ice melts change the weather and freeze the world.

Ice Age directed by Chris Wedge and Carlos Saldanha (20th Century Fox, 2002; Certificate U)
Animated film in which animals try to escape an ice age.

March of the Penguins directed by Luc Jacquet (Warner Home Video, 2006; Certificate U)
Documentary about the lives of the Emperor penguins in the Antarctic.

Websites

http://news.bbc.co.uk/hi/english/static/in_depth/sci_tech/2000/climate_change/
Wide-ranging information about climate change, including children's views on the subject.

www.howstuffworks.com/global-warming.htm
Useful guide to global warming, broken down into easy-to-follow sections.

www.nasa.gov/worldbook/global_warming_worldbook.html
Lots of information and satellite pictures on this site from the National Aeronautics and Space Administration.

www.ncdc.noaa.gov/oa/climate/globalwarming.html
Facts about global warming from the National Oceanic and Atmospheric Administration of the USA, with a useful question and answer section.

Index